GOOD LITTLE KING JOSIAH

2 Kings 22—23 2
Chronicles 34—35 FOR CHILDREN

Written by Mervin Marquardt
Illustrated by Herb Halpern Productions

ARCH Books

Copyright © 1978 CONCORDIA PUBLISHING HOUSE, ST. LOUIS, MISSOURI
MANUFACTURED IN THE UNITED STATES OF AMERICA
ALL RIGHTS RESERVED   ISBN 0-570-06118-0

A long time ago Jerusalem
Was ruled by a wicked king
Who boasted aloud, "I am the best,
So God doesn't mean a thing!"

He taxed his people way too much
    And wasted the money he had
On parties and golden clothes and crowns—
    Whatever the latest fad.

Within the palace lived a boy,
Josiah the prince was he.
Although he was only eight, he was
As good as he could be.

His favorite sport was archery,
    He centered his arrows in;
But always he smiled cheerfully
    Whenever his friends would win.

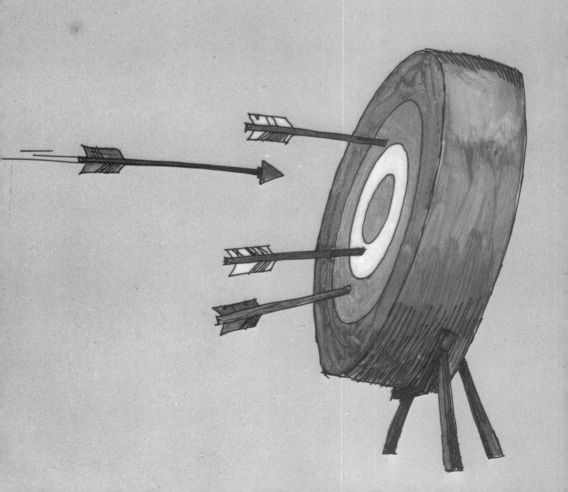

Josiah the prince was happy to be
    A child without a care.
But while he was still an eight-year-old,
    The king was killed somewhere.

"Now Josiah's the king," the people sang,
   "All hail the child king!
Bow down to Josiah's feet and let
   The bells of Jerusalem ring!"

"Josiah, the king"—he liked the sound,
But he didn't know how to rule.
His teachers had never said a thing
About that in the palace school.

So good little King Josiah asked
    Hilkiah the priest, his friend,
To teach him about the government
    And how to govern men.

"Josiah, my king," Hilkiah said,
   The very first thing we do
Is pray on our knees and ask the Lord
   To bless this land anew.

"Josiah and I now ask You, Lord,
A blessing from heaven above:
The wisdom he needs to rule Your land,
The beauty of all Your love."

Hilkiah then told the palace guards,
  "Summon the teachers quick!
Josiah must learn to be a king
  And all about politics."

So the palace guards told the messengers
    Who shouted from the balcony,
"All teachers must come to the palace school
    To teach His Majesty!"

From over the land the teachers came
  To Josiah the child king
To teach him about the land he ruled
  And all about governing.

They taught him to wear a robe and crown,
  To hold his scepter high,
To sit on his throne (which was too big),
  And how to be dignified.

He learned how to wield a sword and shield
    Without hurting himself, of course;
And how to command his generals,
    And how to saddle a horse.

And when he had learned his servants would
　　Bring candy by the crate,
Josiah decided he liked his job,
　　That being the king was great.

The only part he didn't like
   Was the king of the neighboring land;
The king of Assyria made Josiah
   Follow his every command.

"We'll destroy you, Josiah," Assyria said,
  "Unless you agree to pay
Us half of your taxes, and worship all
  Our idols every day."

Josiah the king asked, "Should I serve
   Assyrian gods and throne?
In history I learned King David ruled
   By serving the Lord alone.

"Would David have let our people pray
   To Assyrian gods of stone?
Or have given our money half away?
   This cannot be condoned!"

So good little King Josiah sent
    His servants with this decree:
"Destroy all the idols and serve the Lord
    In every community.

"And send me your taxes which I will use
    To repair the house of the Lord.
We'll clean it and shine it and fix it up right;
    The best we can afford."

So the carpenters came, the goldsmiths too,
   And the stonecutters in a parade
To make the temple beautiful,
   As good as the day it was made.

While they were cleaning a storage room,
   They found a most ancient book
That seemed it was important enough
   for the king to take a look.

When Josiah the king had read it all,
  His face was both happy and sad.
"I'm happy because you found a book
  Nobody remembered we had.

"The book is the Law of the Lord our God
  And promises us His grace.
But it also threatens punishment
  If idols we embrace.

"No wonder we served Assyria,
  That was our punishment.
But here in His Word God promises
  To forgive us if we repent."

Then good little King Josiah called
    For everyone in the land
To join him in worshiping the Lord
    Within the temple grand.

And everyone knew—and still they say—
    "Josiah willingly
Turned to the Lord like no one else;
    A good little king was he."

DEAR PARENTS:

The people of Judah had been living under a series of sever problems from without and within. Tribute to foreign powers such as Babylon and Assyria drained off huge amounts of money. In addition, Judah's kings encouraged foreign idol worship in an effort to "show good faith" to her masters. King Manasseh even burned one of his own sons as sacrifice to the idol Asherah.

When Manasseh died, the people hoped for relief from his son, Amon. When it didn't come in two years, his own counselors slew him and crowned his eight-year-old son Josiah. The full story of Josiah's rule is in 2 Kings 22—23 and 2 Chronicles 34-35.

The point of the story, both here and in the Bible, is that Josiah was "good" because he led his people to worship the Lord as called for in the long-neglected and forgotten book rediscovered during the temple cleansing: the Book of Deuteronomy. Josiah's lasting tribute: "Before him there was no king like him, who turned to the Lord with all his heart and with all his soul and with all his might, according to all the Law of Moses; nor did any like him arise after him" (2 Kings 23:25).

THE EDITOR